NSFW
DIRTY
JOKES
FOR ADULTS

ANOTHER BOOK BY THEM ADULTS

NSFW
OR KIDS!

This book is dedicated to the ADULTS who appreciate a good dirty joke. This book is not for kids, so if you are under 18 reading this - nope - close it now!

ADULTS: Get ready to LOL!
This collection of dirty jokes will have you laughing and covering your face in disbelief. Enjoy and re-tell!
Laughter is the best medicine.

"People think I hate sex.
I don't. I just don't like
things that stop you from seeing
the television properly."
Victoria Wood

TV SEX

A woman went to the doctor
and complained that she was suffering from
knee pains.

"Do you indulge in any activity
that puts a lot of pressure on your knees?"
asked the doctor.

"Every night, my husband and I
have sex on the floor doggy style."

"I see," said the doctor.
"You know, there are plenty of
other sexual positions?"

"Not if you want to watch TV, there ain't!"

What's the difference between a hooker and a drug dealer?

A hooker can wash her crack and sell it again.

Why do women have orgasms?

Just another reason to moan, really.

Why are hurricanes normally named after women?

When they come they're wild and wet, but when they go they take your house and car with them.

**Sex appeal is
50% what you've got and
50% what people
think you've got.**

SEX AFTER DEATH

After 60 years of marriage,
Howard and Velma were inseparable.
They were still sexually active after
all these years, and madly in love.

On night at dinner, the topic of
sex after death came up.
Howard and Velma feared that there
was no after life and no sex
after death.

The couple agreed that if there was
after life, whoever died first would
contact the other spouse and let
them know what's next.

Sadly, Howard died a few years after
the conversation.

One night, Velma was alone and heard a
voice. It was Howard.

"Velma, can you hear me?"

"Howard, is that you?"

"Yes, I've come back to tell you that
there is indeed after life!"

"That's wonderful, Howard.
Tell me, what is it like?"

"Well, I get up in the morning, have sex,
eat breakfast, then off to the golf course.
I then have sex again, bathe in the warm sun,
and then have sex a couple
more times before lunch. Then more sex in the
afternoon before supper.

You'd be proud of all the greens that I'm eating
now a days, Velma.

After dinner, it's sex a few more times, then I
get some much needed sleep. The next day, it
starts all over again!"

"Oh, Howard, it sounds like you
made it to heaven!"

"No, Velma - I am a rabbit
somewhere in Florida."

**Silence doesn't mean
your sexual performance
left her speechless.**

What's the difference between a pregnant woman and a light bulb?

You can unscrew a light bulb.

What do you call a man who cries while he pleasures himself?

A tearjerker.

What do you call a ninety year old man who can still masturbate?

Miracle whip.

The big difference between sex for money and sex for free is that sex for money usually costs a lot less.

GIFTS FOR THE WIFE

A poor man talks to a
rich man around Christmas time.

The rich man says
"I'm getting my wife two gifts this year:
a sports car and a diamond ring.

If she doesn't like the ring she can
drive back to the store to return it."

The poor man thinks for a minute

He says
"Yes, I think I'll do the same.
Two gifts..."

He pauses.

"A pair of slippers and a dildo.

That way if she doesn't like the slippers,
she can go fuck herself."

Whats long, hard and full of seamen?

A submarine.

What's the difference between your dick and a bonus check?

Someone's always willing to blow your bonus.

What did the leper tell the prostitute?

Keep the tip.

"Sex without love is a meaningless experience, but as far as meaningless experiences go its pretty damn good."
Woody Allen

What does one saggy boob say to the other saggy boob?

If we don't get some support, people are going to think we're nuts.

Sex while camping is fucking intents.

What did the banana say to the vibrator?

Why are YOU shaking?
She's going to eat me!

IN THE DARK

A man and a woman started to
have sex in the middle of a dark forest.

After about 15 minutes,
the man finally gets up and says,
"Damn, I wish I had a flashlight!"

The woman says,
"Me too, you've been eating grass
for the past 10 minutes!"

Why do vegetarians give good head?

Because they are use to eating nuts.

What do you call the useless piece of skin on a dick?

The man.

What's the difference between being hungry and being horny?

Where you put the cucumber.

**Women think about
sex every 7 seconds,
just not with you.**

**"Sex is like money;
only too much is enough."**
John Updike

What's the difference between anal and oral sex?

Oral sex makes your day.
Anal makes your hole weak.

What's the difference between a girl and a washing machine?

When a guy dumps a load in the washing machine,
it doesn't follow him around.

What did the toaster say to the slice of bread?

I want you inside of me.

DIRTY BALLS

A guy talking to his doctor about
his physical results.

The doctor says,
"Everything checked out okay,
but I gotta tell you. You have the
dirtiest balls I've ever seen."

The guy returns home,
opens the door, sees his
wife vacuuming busily.

"Honey, I've got to talk to you
about my physical."

"Not now!" she says.
"I'm so busy I don't have time
to wipe my own ass!!"

"That's what I've got to
talk to you about."

"I've got a boyfriend at the moment. Sometimes he's there and sometimes he's not. I prefer it when he's not. Sex is a lot quicker."

Sarah Millican

GARY'S GIFT

It's Gary's birthday.
His wife decided to spice things up this
year for his birthday so takes him to a strip
club as his gift.

They arrive at the club and the
doorman says, "Gary! How are you?"

His wife is puzzled and asks Gary
if he's ever been to this club before.
"Oh no," says Gary.
"He is on my bowling team."

When they are seated, a waitress
tells Gary she will bring him
his usual. Shortly after, a Coors arrives.

His wife is becoming increasingly
uncomfortable and says,
"How did she know that you drink Coors?"

"Oh honey, she's in the ladies bowling league.
We share lanes with them."

A stripper named Bunny
works her way over to their table.

Bunny throws her arms
around Gary and says
"Hey Gary! Want your usual
lap dance, big boy?"

Gary's wife is now furious.

She grabs her purse and
storms out of the club.

Gary follows and spots her getting
into a cab. Before she can
slam the door, he jumps in beside her.

He tries desperately to explain how
the stripper must have mistaken
him for someone else, but his wife
is having none of it.

She is screaming and calling him
every name in the book.

The cabby turns his head
and says,
"Looks like you picked up a
real bitch tonight, Gary.".

"It's been so long since I've had sex I've forgotten who ties up whom."

Joan Rivers

How is a push-up bra like a bag of chips??

As soon as you open it, you realize it's half empty.

How is a woman like a condom?

Both spend more time in your wallet than on your dong.

What do you call an expert fisherman?

A Master Baiter.

CONDOMS

A man walks into the pharmacy
with his 10-year old son.

Waiting for a prescription, they walk
around the store,
passing by a condom display.

"What are these, dad?"
asks the man's son.

The man matter-of-factually replies,
"Those are called condoms son.
Men use them to have safe sex."

"Oh I see," replied the boy.
"Yes, I've heard of that in
health class at school."

He looks over the display and
picks up a package of 3 and asks,
"Why are there 3 in this package?"

The dad replies...

"Those are for high school boys,
one for Friday, one for Saturday,
and one for Sunday."

"Cool" says the boy.

He notices a 6 pack and asks,
"Then who are these for?"

"Those are for college men,"
the dad answers,
"two for Friday, two for Saturday,
and two for Sunday."

"WOW!" exclaimed the boy,
"then who uses THESE?"
he asks, picking up a 12 pack.

With a sigh and a tear in his eye,
the dad replies.
Those are for married men, son.
One for January, one for February,
one for March, one for April..."

HONEYMOON NERVES

A nervous virgin bride was preparing
for her wedding. Running around,
trying to get everything done
before her wedding, the bride's
mom asked how she could help.

"Mom, please go buy me a long
white satin nightgown for the wedding
night. Make sure it's white and long.
Place it carefully in my suitcase so
it won't wrinkle. This is my honeymoon
night, everything must be perfect!"

With all of the wedding tasks,
the bride's mom forgot about
buying the lingerie.
She dashed out and the only thing
she could find was a short pink nightgown.
With no time left, the mom bought it,
throwing it in the bride's suitcase
so that she would have it for
her honeymoon night.

The wedding went off without a hitch!
Now it was time for the honeymoon.

The newly married bride and groom
entered their hotel room.

Both were virgins and filled with anxiety and
nervous about their wedding night. After a few
glasses of champagne, it was time to make the
magic happen.

The bride announced she had a special
outfit for the groom and would
go change in the bathroom.

The groom made her promise
not to peek while he got into bed.

The bride went into the bathroom, opened the
suitcase and saw that her mom had not only
bought the wrong lingerie, she had
thrown it in the suitcase as well!

Upset about the situation, she yelled,
"It's SHORT, PINK, AND WRINKLED!"

An embarrassed groom screamed back
from the bed, "I TOLD YOU NOT TO PEEK!"

BEAVER SHOT

Guy: Doctor, my Girlfriend is pregnant
but we always use protection and
the rubber never broke.
How is it possible?

Doctor : Let me tell you a story...

"There was once a hunter who always
carried a gun wherever he went.

One day he decided to go beaver hunting
and took out his cane instead of his gun.

A beaver suddenly jumped in front of him.
BANG He pulled out his cane and shot the
beaver dead."

Guy: Nonsense! Someone else must have
shot the beaver.

Doctor: Good! You understood the story.
Next patient please...

What did the hurricane say to the coconut tree?

*Hold on to your nuts,
this ain't no ordinary blowjob.*

What did the O say to the Q?

Dude, your dick's hanging out.

What's the difference between a G-spot and a golf ball?

A guy will actually search for a golf ball.

SPAGHETTI

A doctor was having an affair
with his nurse. A few months passed and the
nurse ended up pregnant.

Not wanting his wife to know about the affair
and pregnancy, the doctor offered the nurse
money to go live with her family in Italy, where
she could have the baby and raise it there.

He promised to send her money to
support the child, but his wife could not know
about the situation.

Before leaving the country,the nurse asked the
doctor "How will I let you know when the baby
is born?" He told her to send her a
postcard and just write "spaghetti" on the back.
He assured her that he would take care of all
the expenses. Left with no options,
she returned to her family in Italy.

One afternoon, several months later
the doctor's wife called him at the office.
She told him he had received a very strange
postcard in the mail from Europe and didn't
know who it was from or what it meant.

The doctor told her he would look at it later.

That evening, the doctor went home
and his wife gave him the postcard.
He immediately fell to the floor and
had a heart attack.

The wife called 9-1-1, the ambulance came
and the doctor was rushed to the ER.

At the hospital, a paramedic stayed
with his wife to comfort and keep her
company while her husband was being worked
on. He asked the wife about
what happened before the heart attack,
inquiring if there were any signs or events that
they should know about.

The wife pulled the postcard out of her purse.
"I don't know, he fell to the ground after I
handed him this postcard."

The paramedic puzzled read the postcard
aloud "Spaghetti, Spaghetti, Spaghetti,
Spaghetti - Two with sausage and
meatballs; two without."

NEWLYWED SURPRISE

Newlyweds leave their wedding
and head back to their hotel room.

Both are virgins and have never seen each
other naked before.

After getting to their room, they
start taking their clothes off.

The groom takes it socks and
hoes off and the woman notices that his toes
are severely disfigured.

The man tells his wife,
"I'm sorry I never told you,
but as a child, I had a terrible
disease called toendonitis."

"TOENDONITIS? Are you sure you
don't mean tendonitis?" asks the bride.

"No, trust me! It's a real
thing" said the husband.

Not bothered, they continue to undress.

The husband takes his pants off
and his wife notices his knees
are disfigured as well.

The husband says,
"Yeah, I'm sorry honey. Also as a child
I suffered from kneasles.
Which messed my knees up terribly."

Confused, the woman asks,
"Do you mean measles?!"

Again the man says,
"No trust me, it's a real thing.
You can look it up."

Finally, the man takes his underwear off.

Before he can say anything,
the wife says,
"Let me guess, small cocks?!"

Research shows that 90% of men don't know how to use a condom, these people are called dads.

What's about 6 inches long, is found in a man's pants, and women get so excited over that they often blow it?

A $100 bill.

How is sex like math?

You add a bed, subtract the clothes, divide the legs and hopefully no multiplying.

Why did the snowman drop his pants?

He heard the snowblowers around the corner.

THE FATHER

A guy goes to the supermarket and
notices a beautiful blonde who waves at him
and says hello.

He's rather taken back because he can't place
where he knows her from.

He approaches the blonde and asks
"Do you know me?"

The woman replies,
"I think you're the father of one of my kids."

He thinks back to the only
time he was unfaithful
to his wife and says,

"Oh my God, are you the stripper
from my bachelor party that I screwed on the
pool table with all my buddies watching?"

She replies,
"No, I'm your son's math teacher."

Why do walruses love a tupperware party?

They're always on the lookout for a tight seal.

Owls always look like they just saw a penis for the first time.

What's the best part about gardening?

Getting down and dirty with your hoes.

My girlfriend caught me blowing my dick with the air dryer, and asked what I was doing.

Apparently "heating your dinner"
wasn't a good answer.

The bigger your feet, the bigger our dick. The bigger your car, the smaller your dick.

No wonder we are scared of clowns.

What do you call an anal sex toy that is constantly self advertising?

A shameless plug.

DIRTY PENGUIN

A penguin is driving to the mall when all of a sudden his engine starts running rough and smoke is coming out from under the hood.

He pulls into an auto repair shop right next to the mall. The mechanic says he'll be glad to take a look at it and to come back in a few hours.

The penguin says fine, and walks to the mall to do some shopping and gets an ice cream.

2 hours later he returns to the see the mechanic. The penguin asks the mechanic, "What's wrong?" The mechanic says, "It looks like you blew a seal."

The penguin says, "No, that's just ice cream."

The mechanic goes to the register to ring up the penguin for the repairs. He gives it his price. The penguin mutters to himself that it was a little high and the mechanic said "come again?" The penguin yelled "ITS JUST ICE CREAM!

LABOR PAINS

A married couple went to the hospital
to have their baby delivered.

When they arrived, the doctor said he had in-
vented a new machine that would transfer a
portion of the mother's pain to the baby's father. The doctor asked if they were willing to
be apart of the trial. The husband agreed so
the doctor setup the pain transfer.

The wife's labor started to progress so the doctor set the pain transfer to 10%,
for starters, explaining that even 10%
was probably more pain the father had ever
experienced before.

However, as the labor progressed,
the husband felt fine and asked the
doctor to go ahead and "kick it up a notch."

The doctor then adjusted the machine
to 20% pain transfer.

The husband was still feeling fine.
The doctor checked the husband's
blood pressure and was amazed at how well
he was doing at this point!

The doctor asked the husband if he
wanted to increase the pain transfer.
Seeing that he was feeling well, he agreed.

The pain transfer was obviously
helping out the wife considerably,
the husband encouraged the doctor
to transfer ALL the pain to him.

In no time, the wife delivered a healthy
baby girl with nearly NO PAIN!
The couple was ecstatic and the doctor was
baffled at how well the trial went.

When they got home, the mailman
was found dead on the porch.

BABY KNOWS

A baby was born that was so
advanced that he could talk.

He looked around the delivery room
and saw his mama"

He looked at his mother and asked,
"Are you my mother?"

"Yes, I am,"
she said.

"Thank you for taking such good care of me
before I was born"
he said.

He then looked at his father and asked
"Are you my father?"

"Yes, I am," his father answered.

The baby motioned him close,
then poked him on the forehead with
his index finger 5 times, saying
"I want you to know that THAT HURTS!"

**Remember, if you
smoke after sex
you're doing it too fast
and need more lubricant.**

VIAGRA

A man walks into a pharmacy
and says to the pharmacist,
"Listen, I have 3 women coming
over tonight. I've never had three
women at once! I need something to keep
me ready and keep me potent."

The pharmacist leans over to the
man and tells him he has him covered,
but he can't tell anyone.

He then reaches under the counter, unlocks
the bottom drawer and takes out a small card-
board box marked with a label
Extra Strength Viagra and says,
"Here, if you eat this,
you'll go nuts for twelve hours."

The man asks for 3 boxes.

"3 boxes? Are you sure?"
asks the pharmacist.

"YES!" said the man as he quickly hands over cash and runs out of the pharmacy.

The next day, the guy walks into the same pharmacy. He slowly limps up to the pharmacist and pulls down his pants.

The pharmacist looks in horror as he notices the man's penis is black and blue, appearing mangled with chunks of skin are hanging off in some places.

In a pained voice, the man moans out, "Gimme a bottle of Deep Heat."

The pharmacist replies in horror, "You can't put Deep Heat on that!"

The man replies, "Don't worry, it's not for my penis. It's for my arms, the girls didn't show up."

RED TOMATOES

A woman is having a hard time getting
her tomatoes to ripen so she goes to her
neighbor with her problem.

The neighbor says,
"All you have to do is go out at midnight and
dance around in the garden naked for a
few minutes, and the tomatoes
will become so embarrassed,
they will blush bright red."

The woman goes out at
midnight and dances around
her garden naked for a few minutes.

The next morning, the neighbor
comes over to the woman's house and asks
the woman if her tomatoes have turned red.

The woman says
"No, they're still green,
but I noticed the cucumbers
grew 4 inches!"

Sex with 3 people is
called a threesome.

Sex with 2 people is
called a twosome.

That explains why they
call you handsome.

BEFORE HE DIES

Mark returned from a doctor's visit
and told his wife Alma that the doctor said he
only had 24 hours to live.

Wiping away her tears, he asked her to make
love with him.

Of course she agreed and
they made passionate love.

6 hours later, Mark went to her again.
"Honey, now I only have 18 hours left to live.
Maybe we could make love again?"

Sarah agreed and again they made love.

Later, Mark was getting into bed
when he realized he now had only
8 hours of life left.

He touched Sarah's shoulder and said,
"Honey Please?
Just one more time before I die."

She agreed, then afterwards she
rolled over and fell asleep.

Mark, however, heard the clock
ticking in his head, and he
tossed and turned until he was
down to only 4 more hours.

He tapped his wife on the
shoulder to wake her up.

"Honey, I only have 4 hours left!
Could we...?"

His wife sat up abruptly,
turned to him and said,
"Listen Mark, I have to
get up in the morning
to plan your funeral and
you don't have to get up!"

Two eggs are boiling in a pan.

One says
"I've got a huge crack."

The other replies,
"Stop teasing me,
I'm not hard yet."

$2000 SEX

A boss said to his secretary I want
to have SEX with you I will make it very fast.
I'll throw $1000 on the floor, by the time you
bend down to pick it I'll be done.

The secretary thought for a moment
then called her boyfriend and told
him the story.

Her boyfriend then said to her, do it but
"Ask him for $2000, pick up the money
so fast he wouldn't even have enough
time to undressed himself."
So she agreed.

Half an hour goes by, the boyfriend
calls his girlfriend and asks
what happened?

She responds,
"The bastard used coins
I'm still picking up the money and
he is still fucking!"

How do you
spot a blind man
on a nude beach?

It"s not hard.

Women wake up
yawning and men
wake up with an erection.

Coincidence? I think not!

What did the elephant ask
the naked man?

How do you breathe out of that thing?

**The worst things
about giving
a man
a blow job
is the view.**

BACK DOOR

I was banging this lady on her
kitchen table when we heard
the front door open.

She said, "It's my husband!
Quick, try the back door!"

Thinking back, I really should
have ran but you don't get
offers like that every day.

What do you get when you mix birth control and LSD?

A trip without kids.

How is sex like a game of bridge?

If you have a great hand, you don't need a partner.

What do you call a herd of cows masturbating?

Beef strokin' off.

"I've never laughed a woman in to bed, but I've laughed one out of bed many times."

Jack Whitehall

WIFI

A man who travels full-time
received text from his neighbor:

Hey I am using your wife...

I am using day and night...

I am using when u r not present at home...

In fact I am using more than U R using...

I confess this because now I feel
very much guilt...

Hope U will accept my sincere apologies...

The man called home pissed. His wife
was in disbelief that he would accuse her of
anything of the such.

A few minutes later he
received another message…

Sorry man, just saw the text to speech
auto-corrected WIFI to WIFE.
Again, sorry for using your WIFI so much.

THE DILDO

A man and woman had been married
for 30 years, and in those 30 years,
they always left the lights off
when having sex.

He was embarrassed and scared
that he couldn't please her, so he
always used a big dildo on her.

All these years she had no clue.

One day, she decided to reach over
and flip the light switch on and
saw that he was using a dildo.

She said,
"I knew it, asshole,
explain the dildo!"

He said,
"Explain the kids!

What is the difference between your wife and your job?

After five years your job still sucks.

How do you make your girlfriend scream during sex?

Call and tell her about it.

I tried phone sex
once, but the
holes were
too small.

DREAMING

It's guy's ski weekend at the ski resort. Upon arriving at the resort, the group discovers that the 2 queen bed and a couch suite isn't available.

The trio ends up with the only room left, a single king bed.

The next morning, the guy on the right side of the bed tells his friends about a dream he had that he was getting an amazing hand job.

The guy on the left side of the bed says "Wow, thats weird, I dreamed I got an amazing hand job too!"

The guy in the middle says "Hmm. Thats funny! I dreamed I was skiing."

30 SECONDS

A guy and his wife are sitting
and watching a boxing match on television.

The husband sighs and complains,
"This is disappointing. It only lasted
for 30 seconds!"

"Good," replied his wife.
"Now you know how I always feel."

"Recently my girlfriend asked me if I was having sex behind her back and I replied, 'Yes, who did you think it was?'"

Jimmy Carr

Now I know why they call it a beaver, because it wants your wood.

YOUNG COCK

A farmer buys a young cock.

As soon as he gets the young cock
home, it is fucking all of the
farmer's 150 hens.

The farmer is impressed and
was surprised to find him the next day,
fucking the ducks and all of the geese!

Sadly later that day, the farmer finds
the young cock lying on the ground,
half-dead with vultures circling overhead.

The farmer says,
"You deserved it, you horny bastard!"

The cock opens one eye,
points up and says
"Shhh.... they are about to land!"

THANKS

A female secretary got an
expensive pen as a gift from her boss.

She sent him a
'Thank you note' by email.

The boss's wife read the email and
filed for divorce.

The email said:
Your penis wonderful and I
enjoyed using it last night.
It has extraordinary smooth flow
and a firm stroke.

I loved its perfect size and grip.
Felt like I was in heaven when using it.
Thanks a lot.

Moral of the story.
A "space" is an essential part
of English grammar.

VAGINA:
the box a
penis comes in.

My girlfriend told me to go out and get something that makes her look sexy... so I got drunk.

HAPPY BIRTHDAY

Why did I get divorced?
Well, last week was my birthday.

My wife didn't wish me a happy birthday.
My parents forgot and so did my kids.
I went to work and even my colleagues
didn't wish me a happy birthday.

As I entered my office, my secretary said,
"Happy birthday, boss!" I felt so special.

She asked me out for lunch. After lunch,
she invited me to her apartment.

We went to her place and she said,
"Do you mind if I go into the
bedroom for a minute?"

"Okay," I said.

She came out 5 minutes later
with a birthday cake, my wife
my parents, my kids, my friends, and
my colleagues all yelling, "SURPRISE!!!
while I was waiting on the sofa... *naked.*

SO WET

"Give it to me! Give it to me!"
she yelled.

"I'm so wet, give it to me now!"

She could scream all she wanted to.

I was keeping the umbrella.

**Sex takes up the least
amount of time
and causes the most
amount of trouble.**

**Unexpected sex
is a great way to
be woken up,
unless you are in prison.**

PULL

An old couple was laying in bed
watching TV.

The elderly man turns over
and tells his wife
"If you want to have sex,
pull on my dick once.
If you don't want to have sex,
pull on my dick one hundred times."

6 KIDS

A man boards a plane with 6 kids.

After they get settled in their seats,
a woman sitting across the aisle leans
over to him and asks,
"Are all of those kids yours?"

He replies,
"No. I work for a condom company.
These are just a few of
the customer complaints."

"Don't kid yourself"
would be a great slogan
for a condom company.

THE WIFE

Two men visit a prostitute.

The first man goes into the bedroom.
He comes out ten minutes later and says,
"Heck. My wife is better than that."

The second man goes in.
He comes out ten minutes later and says,
"You know? Your wife IS better."

My wife told
me sex is better
on holiday, that wasn't
a very nice postcard
to receive.

Women might be able
to fake orgasms,
but men can fake a
whole relationship.

2040

There is more money being
spent on breast implants and Viagra today,
than on Alzheimer's research.

This means that by 2040,
there should be a large elderly
population with perky boobs,
huge erections, and absolutely
no recollection of what to do with them.

RUBBER

A kid walks up to his mom and asks,
"Mom, can I go
bungee jumping?"

The mom says
"No, you were born because of
a broken rubber and I don't
want you to go out the same way!"

**If a woman sleeps
with 10 men she's a slut,
but if a man does it,
he is definitely gay.**

Can't spell ADVERTISEMENTS without semen between the tits.

SHORT STORY CONTEST

Contest in a girl's college:
write a short story which
contains religion, sex and mystery.

Winner's story:
"Oh god, I am pregnant,
I wonder who did it."

THE PILL

A woman goes to the doctor complaining that her husband is losing interest in sex. The doctor tells her about an experimental pill, but warns it hasn't been thoroughly tested. Desperate for sex, she agrees.

That night, she follows the doctor's orders to put the pill in his mashed potatoes and reports back to him the results.

The next day, the woman shows up to the doctor's office excited. "Doc, that pill is amazing! I put it in the potatoes, just like you said to! It wasn't five minutes later that he jumped up, threw all the food and dishes onto the floor, grabbed me, ripped all my clothes off, and ravaged me right there on the table!"

The doctor says, "I'm sorry, the pill is still in testing. Let me see if we can get some funds to help pay for any damages."

"Nah," she says, "That's okay. We're never going back to that restaurant, anyways."

"I'm taking Viagra and drinking prune juice - I don't know if I'm coming or going."

Rodney Dangerfield

WEIGHT LOSS

An overweight man is watching TV.
A commercial comes on featuring a weight loss
program with a guarantee weight loss of
10 pounds in a week.

The man at his wits end and tired of being
overweight, he decides to sign up.

The next morning, his doorbell rings.
A beautiful woman is at the door.
She is wearing nothing but running shoes and
a sign around her neck that reads "If you can
catch me, you can have me."
Before he knows it, she takes off running.

He tries to catch her, but is unable.
This continues each day for a week. At the end
of 7 days, the man had lost 10 pounds! Happy
with his successful weight loss, he decided to
sign up for phase 2 of the weight loss program
that guarantees a 15 pound weight loss!

The next day, his doorbell rings.
ANOTHER beautiful woman is at the door that
is even more beautiful than the first!

Again, he tries to catch her each
morning for a week, with no success
but does lose 15 pounds!

So thrilled with his weight loss success, the
man decides to sign up for phase 3
of the program guaranteeing a weight loss of
25 pounds in a week!

The weight loss program came with
a warning requiring a waiver to be signed
because of the intensity of phase 3.

Just like in phase 1 and phase 2,
his doorbell rings - but this time there isn't a
beautiful woman at the door. Instead, there is
a bulky 300 pound muscle man standing at the
door with nothing but a pair of running shoes, a
raging erection and a sign that says,
"If I can catch you, you are MINE!"

Needless to say, the phase 3
of the program was a success.
Instead of the 25 pound weight loss
that week, he lost 33 pounds.

"I can remember when the air was clean and sex was dirty."

George Burns

UNDER THE PILLOW

Grandma and Grandpa were
visiting their kids overnight .

When Grandpa found a bottle of Viagra in his
son's medicine cabinet, he asked about using
one of the pills.

The son said,
"I don't think you should take one Dad, they're
very strong and very expensive."

"How much?" asked Grandpa.
"$10.00 a pill," answered the son.
"I don't care," said Grandpa,

"I'd still like to try one, and before we leave in
the morning, I'll put the
money under the pillow. "

Later the next morning, the son found $110
under the pillow.

He called Grandpa and said,
"I told you each pill was $10, not $110.
"I know," said Grandpa.
"The hundred is from Grandma!"

HOLIDAY TATTOOS

It was Christmas Eve and a woman
came home to her husband after a day of busy
shopping and errands.

That night when she was
getting undressed for bed, and her
husband noticed bandages on
the inside of her thighs.

"What is that?"
he asked.

She said, "I visited the tattoo parlor today.
On the inside of one thigh I had them tattoo
'Merry Christmas,'
and on the inside of the
other thigh they tattooed
'Happy New Year.'"

Perplexed, he asked,
"Why did you do that?"

"Well," she replied,
"now you can't complain that there's
never anything to eat between
Christmas and New Years!"

What's worse than waking up at a party and finding a penis drawn on your face?

Finding out it was traced.

What's the difference between a bitch and a whore?

A whore sleeps with everybody at the party, and a bitch sleeps with everybody at the party except you.

What's the difference between your boyfriend and a condom?

Condoms have evolved. They're not so thick and insensitive anymore.

Anal intercourse
is for
assholes.

I may not be getting laid tonight, but I'm definitely banging my snooze button in the morning.

How is life
like a penis?

Your girlfriend makes it hard.

DOORBELL RINGER

A woman places a post on a local website.

"Looking for a man with 3 qualifications:

1. He won't beat me up.
2. He won't run away from me.
3. MUST BE GREAT IN BED!"

2 days later her doorbell rings.

"Hi, I'm Tim. I have no arms
so I won't beat you
and no legs so I won't run away."

"What makes you think you
are great in bed?"
the woman retorts.

Tim replies,
"I rang the doorbell, didn't I?"

What do prostitutes and bungee jumping have in common?

They both cost $100 and if the rubber breaks your screwed!

"My wife is a sex object. Every time I ask for sex, she objects."
Les Dawson

Do you know what 6.9 is?

A good thing screwed up by a period.

4 LEGS

A wife comes home late one night.
Not wanting to wake her husband, she quietly
opens the door to the master bedroom.

Instead of the lump her husband usually
forms in bed, she sees 4 LEGS instead of her
husband's 2 legs.

Upset, she grabs a baseball bat
and starts hitting the blanket
as hard as she can.

Once she is done, the woman
goes to the kitchen for a drink. As she enters
the kitchen, she was shocked to
see her husband standing
there reading a magazine.

He greets her.

"Hi, honey! Your parents came
in for a surprise visit. I hope it's okay
that they stay in our bedroom.
Did you say hello?"

LATEX

A gynecologist notices that a
new patient is nervous.

Trying to ease the tension,
while the doctor is putting on the
latex gloves, he asks her if she knows
how they make latex gloves.

The patient says no.

The doctor says,
"There is a plant in Mexico full of
latex that people of various hand
sizes dip their hands into and let them dry."

She does not crack a smile,
but later she laughs.

The doctor says,
"What's so funny?"

She says,
"I'm imagining how
they make condoms."

I was masturbating today and my hand fell asleep, that's got to be the ultimate rejection.

How do you tell the difference between an oral and a rectal thermometer?

By the taste.

My wife suggested we should try some role reversal in bed so I told her I have a headache.

What's the difference between a hockey player and a hippie chick?

The hockey player takes a shower after three periods.

GREAT SEX

Hanging out at the bar,
a man is talking to his friend and says,
"I don't know what to get my wife
for her birthday. She has everything,
and besides, she can afford to buy anything
she wants. I'm stumped."

His friend has an idea.
"Why don't you make up a gift
certificate that says she can have 2 hours
of great sex, any way she wants it.
She'll probably be thrilled!"

The man loves the idea and gifts
his wife with the certificate.

The next day, his buddy asks,
"Well, did you take my suggestion?
How did it turn out?"

"She loved it. She jumped up,
thanked me, kissed me on the mouth,
and ran out the door yelling,
'I'll see you in two hours!'"

50 YEARS LATER

An elderly couple are celebrating their
50th anniversary, eating dinner in the
courtyard at the restaurant
where they first met.

During dinner they began reminiscing.
"Honey, do you remember when we made love
against that fence over there?" the man asks.

"Of course", replies the woman,
"That was a night to remember!
We should do it again, for old times' sake."

The old man grins with excitement!
The couple sneaks away from
dinner and takes go over to the
fence where they first had made love.

Their waiter, having overheard
the discussion. In disbelief,
he decides he has to see
if they are actually going to do it.

The waiter follows the couple
and watches from a distance.

He sees the old woman lift her dress
and the old man drop his trousers.

As she leans against the fence,
they immediately start screwing
like jackhammers, frantically pounding
into each other.

After going at it for a good while,
they collapse back onto the ground
and lay there gasping.

The waiter runs over in disbelief and states,
"I'm sorry to seem like a voyeur,
but that was some of the most amazing
sex I've ever seen! I can't believe you 2
have been fucking like that for 50 years!"

The old man replies,
"We haven't. 50 years ago that
fence wasn't electrified."

**Without nipples,
breasts would
be pointless.**

What do boobs and toys have in common?

*They were both originally
made for kids,
but daddies end
up playing with them.*

Why does Santa Claus have such a big sack?

He only comes once a year.

What do the mafia and pussies have in common?

*One slip of the tongue,
and you're in deep shit.*

PRETEND MARRIAGE

A man and a woman who had
never met before found themselves
assigned to the same sleeping room
on a trans-continental train.

Though initially embarrassed
and uneasy over sharing a room, they were
both very tired and fell asleep quickly.

The man slept on the top bunk,
and the woman asleep in the lower.

At 1:00 AM, the man leaned down
and gently woke the woman saying,
"Ma'am, I'm sorry to bother you, but would you
be willing to reach into the closet to get me a
second blanket? I'm awfully cold."

"I have a better idea," she replied.
"Just for tonight, let's pretend
we're married."

"Wow! That's a great idea!"
he exclaimed.
"Good," she replied.

"Get your own fucking blanket."

After a moment of silence, he farted.

What is the difference between kinky and perverted?

Kinky is when you tickle your lover's ass with a feather. Perverted is when you use the whole chicken.

What's the difference between a man and a margarita?

A margarita hits the spot every time.

What's the difference between a lentil and a chick-pea?

I wouldn't pay $20 to have a lentil on my face.

Scientists have proven that there are two things in the air that have been known to cause women to get pregnant: their legs.

"Sex is a two-way treat."

Franklin Jones

THE OFFICE BLONDE

Three secretaries all left the office
for lunch together.

As they got in the elevator,
they noticed a small pool of
white-ish fluid on the floor.

The brunette said,
"Ew! Is that semen?"

The redhead leaned closer,
then said,
"Yep, definitely semen"

The blonde leaned down and
scooped up a fingerful.

After tasting it she said,
"Well, it's certainly not anyone
in our office."

WHALE THEN

A male whale and a female whale
were swimming off the coast of Japan
when they noticed a whaling ship.

The male whale recognized it as
the same ship that had harpooned
his father many years earlier.

He said to the female whale,
"Lets both swim under the ship and
blow out of our air holes
at the same time and it should
cause the ship to turn over and sink."

They tried it and sure enough,
the ship turned over and quickly sank.

Soon however, the whales realized
the sailors had jumped overboard and
were swimming to the safety of shore.

The male whale was enraged that
they were going to get away and
told the female whale,
"Let's swim after them and gobble
them up before they reach the shore."

At this point, he realized the female
was becoming reluctant to follow him.

"Look," she said,
"I went along with the blow job,
but I absolutely refuse to
swallow the seamen."

What's the difference between a tire and 365 used condoms?

One's a Goodyear.
The other's a great year.

"I admit, I have a tremendous sex drive. My boyfriend lives forty miles away. "
Phyllis Diller

What does a perverted frog say?

Rubbit

SMART HORSE

Steve is sleeping with a married woman.
At here house, she is nervous.

"You should leave now.
My husband will be home soon",
said the woman.

"Don't worry, I brought my trained
smart horse. He is outside. If I just blow my
whistle and jump out the window,
he will catch me, allowing me to get away"

There was a knock on the door and
Steve panicked. He quickly blew his
whistle, then jumped out the window.

The woman went to answer the
door and found Steve's horse
standing in the doorway.

"It's raining heavily outside.
I came to tell Steve that I'll
be waiting for him in the living room."
said the horse.

CRABS OR LOBSTER?

A man goes to a $10 prostitute
and contracts crabs.

He goes back to the
prostitute and complains.

The prostitute laughs
and responds,
"What do you expect for $10?
Lobster?"

What is the difference between a Genealogist and a Gynecologist?

A Genealogist looks up your family tree.
A Gynecologist looks up your family bush.

"I believe that sex is one of the most beautiful, natural, wholesome things that money can buy."
Steve Martin

What did the penis say to the vagina?

Don't make me come in there!

Made in the USA
Monee, IL
08 November 2022